Hear Me

A Prayerbook for Orthodox Teens

compiled and edited
by Annalisa Boyd

CONCILIAR PRESS MINISTRIES,
CHESTERTON, INDIANA

D1228027

Hear Me:
A Prayerbook for Orthodox Teens

Prayers are adapted from original ancient sources by the author.

Scripture quotations are from the New King James Version of the Bible, © 1982
by Thomas Nelson, Inc., Nashville, Tennessee, and are used by permission.

Published by   Conciliar Press
                    A division of Conciliar Media Ministries
                    P.O. Box 748
                    Chesterton, IN 46304

Printed in the United States of America

ISBN 10: 1-888212-93-4
ISBN 13: 978-1-888212-93-8

The Good, the Bad, and the Family—

Warning: Life Under Pressure—

Declaration of Dependence—

HEAR ME
an introduction
to the prayer book

I sought the Lord, and He heard me,
And delivered me from all my fears.
—Psalm 34:4

Welcome to your personal prayer book. May you find joy and peace within its pages. As youth, you have entered an exciting time of life. You are able to exercise more freedom in your daily activities and in your faith. You may not be aware of it, but right at this moment you are developing patterns for living that will follow you through the teen years and into adulthood. Patterns for developing friendships. Work and study patterns. Even patterns for your spiritual life.

Prayer is a valuable pattern to establish, and you will be challenged as you pursue your personal prayers and quiet times with Christ and His saints. The world offers so many distractions, but a well-established prayer time is like a tree with strong roots. When the winds, or trials and temptations of life, come, you will stand firm.

In this book you will find prayers and encouragement for many areas of your life. Written prayers are valuable tools which, in time, become prayers of the heart, not just the mouth. Adding your own personal thoughts, praise, and confession makes praying even more meaningful.

May these prayers open your heart to your Savior and bless you as you grow in the love and knowledge of our Lord Jesus Christ. May you know that you have a God who hears you!

On the Front Lines
daily prayers

Who is this King of glory?
The LORD strong and mighty,
The LORD mighty in battle.
—Psalm 24:8

When preparing for a battle, it is important to go to your commander, seeking his direction and listening to his plan of attack. It is no different in our Christian walk. Trials and temptations assail us daily, and if we are not armed and prepared through close communication with our Commander, we will fall in battle. We arm ourselves through extensive training in prayer and union with the Lord through the sacraments. Through prayer we are able to recognize the enemy and false teachings, which can be deadly landmines resulting in unnecessary casualties. God doesn't wait for you to fall, either; He is right there with you in the heat of battle.

> *Do not rush one prayer after another, but say them with orderly deliberation, as one addressing a great person for a favor. Do not just pay attention to the words, but rather let the mind be in the heart, standing before the Lord in full awareness of His presence, in full consciousness of His greatness and grace and justice.*
> —Saint Theophan the Recluse

+ Morning Prayers

The Trisagion Prayers

In the Name of the Father, and of the Son, and of the Holy Spirit. Amen.

Glory to Thee, our God, glory to Thee.

O Heavenly King, O Comforter, the Spirit of truth, who art in all places and fillest all things; Treasury of good things and Giver of Life: Come and dwell in us, and cleanse us from every stain, and save our souls, O gracious Lord.

Holy God, Holy Mighty, Holy Immortal, have mercy on us.
Holy God, Holy Mighty, Holy Immortal, have mercy on us.
Holy God, Holy Mighty, Holy Immortal, have mercy on us.

Glory to the Father, and to the Son, and to the Holy Spirit, both now and ever and unto ages of ages. Amen.

All-holy Trinity, have mercy on us. Lord, cleanse us from our sins. Master, pardon our iniquities. Holy God, visit and heal our infirmities for Thy Name's sake.

Lord, have mercy, Lord, have mercy, Lord, have mercy.

Glory to the Father, and to the Son, and to the Holy Spirit, both now and ever and unto ages of ages. Amen.

Our Father, who art in heaven, hallowed be Thy Name; Thy Kingdom come; Thy will be done on earth as it is in heaven. Give us this day our daily bread; and forgive us our trespasses, as we forgive those who trespass against us; and lead us not into temptation, but deliver us from evil.

For Thine is the Kingdom, and the power, and the glory, of the Father, and of the Son, and of the Holy Spirit, now and ever and unto ages of ages. Amen.

A Prayer for the Beginning of the Day
by Saint Philaret of Moscow

O Lord, grant me to greet this new day in peace. Help me in all things to humbly rely upon Your holy will. In every hour of the day, reveal Your will to me. Bless my dealings with all who surround me. Teach me to treat all that comes to me throughout the day with peace of soul and the firm conviction that Your will governs all. In all I do and say, guide my thoughts and feelings. In unforeseen events, let me not forget that all are sent by You. Teach me to act firmly and wisely, without embittering or embarrassing others. Give me the strength to bear the fatigue of the coming day with all that it shall bring. Direct my will, teach me to pray, and pray Yourself within me. Amen.

A Portion of the Breastplate Prayer
by Saint Patrick

I arise today, through God's strength to pilot me:
God's might to uphold me, God's wisdom to guide me,
God's eye to look before me, God's ear to hear me,
God's word to speak for me, God's hand to guard me,
God's way to lie before me, God's shield to protect me,
God's host to secure me:
Against snares of devils, against temptations of vices,
Against inclinations of nature, against everyone who
Shall wish me ill, afar and near, alone and in a crowd.

Christ with me, Christ before me,
Christ behind me, Christ in me,
Christ beneath me, Christ above me,
Christ on my right,
Christ on my left,
Christ in breadth,
Christ in length,
Christ in height,
Christ in the heart of every man who thinks of me,
Christ in the mouth of every man who speaks of me,
Christ in every eye that sees me,
Christ in every ear that hears me.

Salvation is of the Lord. Salvation is of the Lord.
Salvation is of Christ.
May Thy Salvation, O Lord, be ever with us.

Psalm 5:1-3

Give ear to my words, O Lord,
Consider my meditation.
Give heed to the voice of my cry,
My King and my God,
For to You I will pray.
My voice You shall hear in the morning, O Lord;
In the morning I will direct it to You,
And I will look up.

A Prayer to the Holy Trinity

Arising from sleep I thank You, O holy Trinity, because of the riches of your goodness and longsuffering. In Your compassion You raised me up, as I lay in hopelessness, that in the morning I might sing the glories of Your Majesty. Guide the eyes of my understanding; open my mouth to receive Your words; teach me Your commandments; help me to do Your will, confessing You from my heart, singing and praising Your All-holy Name: of the Father, and of the Son, and of the Holy Spirit, now and ever and unto ages of ages. Amen.

The Creed

I believe in one God, the Father Almighty, Maker of heaven and earth, and of all things visible and invisible.

And in one Lord Jesus Christ, the Son of God, the Only-begotten, begotten of the Father before all worlds; Light of Light, very God of very God, begotten, not made; of one essence with the Father, by whom all things were made:

Who for us men and for our salvation came down from heaven, and was incarnate of the Holy Spirit and the Virgin Mary, and became man;

And was crucified also for us under Pontius Pilate, and suffered and was buried;

And the third day He rose again, according to the Scriptures; And ascended into heaven, and sits at the right hand of the Father;

And He shall come again with glory to judge the living and the dead, whose Kingdom shall have no end.

And I believe in the Holy Spirit, the Lord and Giver of Life, who proceeds from the Father, who with the Father and the Son together is worshipped and glorified, who spoke by the Prophets;

And I believe in One Holy Catholic and Apostolic Church. I acknowledge one Baptism for the remission of sins. I look for the resurrection of the dead and the life of the world to come. Amen.

Feel free to add your own personal prayers, praises, and requests here.

Through the prayers of our holy Fathers, Lord Jesus Christ our God, have mercy upon me and save me. Amen.

+ Midday Prayers

The Trisagion Prayers

In the Name of the Father, and of the Son, and of the Holy Spirit. Amen.

Glory to Thee, our God, glory to Thee.

O Heavenly King, O Comforter, the Spirit of truth, who art in all places and fillest all things; Treasury of good things and Giver of Life: Come and dwell in us, and cleanse us from every stain, and save our souls, O gracious Lord.

Holy God, Holy Mighty, Holy Immortal, have mercy on us.
Holy God, Holy Mighty, Holy Immortal, have mercy on us.
Holy God, Holy Mighty, Holy Immortal, have mercy on us.

Glory to the Father, and to the Son, and to the Holy Spirit, both now and ever and unto ages of ages. Amen.

All-holy Trinity, have mercy on us. Lord, cleanse us from our sins. Master, pardon our iniquities. Holy God, visit and heal our infirmities for Thy Name's sake.

Lord, have mercy, Lord, have mercy, Lord, have mercy.

Glory to the Father, and to the Son, and to the Holy Spirit, both now and ever and unto ages of ages. Amen.

Our Father, who art in heaven, hallowed be Thy Name; Thy Kingdom come; Thy will be done on earth as it is in heaven. Give us this day our daily bread; and forgive us our trespasses, as we forgive those who trespass against us; and lead us not into temptation, but deliver us from evil.

For Thine is the Kingdom, and the power, and the glory, of the Father, and of the Son, and of the Holy Spirit, now and ever and unto ages of ages. Amen.

Troparion for the Sixth Hour
O Christ my God, who at this hour stretched out Your loving arms upon the cross so that all men might be gathered unto You, help me and save me as I cry out to You: Glory to You, O Lord.

> *Prayer helps us develop a living relationship with the Lord, so feel free to add your own prayers, praises, and requests here.*

Through the prayers of our holy Fathers, Lord Jesus Christ our God, have mercy upon me and save me. Amen.

+ Evening Prayers

The Trisagion Prayers
In the Name of the Father, and of the Son, and of the Holy Spirit. Amen.

Glory to Thee, our God, glory to Thee.

O Heavenly King, O Comforter, the Spirit of truth, who art in all places and fillest all things; Treasury of good things and Giver of Life: Come and dwell in us, and cleanse us from every stain, and save our souls, O gracious Lord.

Holy God, Holy Mighty, Holy Immortal, have mercy on us.

Holy God, Holy Mighty, Holy Immortal, have mercy on us.
Holy God, Holy Mighty, Holy Immortal, have mercy on us.

Glory to the Father, and to the Son, and to the Holy Spirit, both now and ever and unto ages of ages. Amen.

All-holy Trinity, have mercy on us. Lord, cleanse us from our sins. Master, pardon our iniquities. Holy God, visit and heal our infirmities for Thy Name's sake.

Lord, have mercy, Lord, have mercy, Lord, have mercy.

Glory to the Father, and to the Son, and to the Holy Spirit, both now and ever and unto ages of ages. Amen.

Our Father, who art in heaven, hallowed be Thy Name; Thy Kingdom come; Thy will be done on earth as it is in heaven. Give us this day our daily bread; and forgive us our trespasses, as we forgive those who trespass against us; and lead us not into temptation, but deliver us from evil.

For Thine is the Kingdom, and the power, and the glory, of the Father, and of the Son, and of the Holy Spirit, now and ever and unto ages of ages. Amen.

Troparia of Thanksgiving

Now that the day has come to a close, I thank You, O Lord, and I ask that the evening with the night may be sinless; grant this to me, O Savior, and save me.

Glory to the Father, and to the Son, and to the Holy Spirit.

Now that the day has passed, I glorify You, O Master, and I ask that the evening with the night may be without wrongdoing; grant this to me, O Savior, and save me.

Both now and ever and unto ages of ages. Amen.

Now that the day has run its course, I praise You, O Holy One, and I ask that the evening with the night may be undisturbed; grant this to me, O Savior, and save me.

Lord, have mercy. *(12 times)*

A Prayer For Forgiveness

O Lord, our God, if during this day I have sinned, whether in word or deed or thought, forgive me all, for You are good and You love mankind. Grant me peaceful and undisturbed sleep, and deliver me from the temptations of the evil one. Raise me up again in the morning that I may glorify You; for You are blessed, with Your Only-begotten Son and Your All-holy Spirit, now and ever and unto ages of ages. Amen.

The Creed

I believe in one God, the Father Almighty, Maker of heaven and earth, and of all things visible and invisible.

And in one Lord Jesus Christ, the Son of God, the Only-begotten, begotten of the Father before all worlds; Light of Light, very God of very God, begotten, not made; of one essence with the Father, by whom all things were made:

Who for us men and for our salvation came down from heaven, and was incarnate of the Holy Spirit and the Virgin Mary, and became man;

And was crucified also for us under Pontius Pilate, and suffered and was buried;

And the third day He rose again, according to the Scriptures; And ascended into heaven, and sits at the right hand of the Father;

And He shall come again with glory to judge the living and the dead, whose Kingdom shall have no end.

And I believe in the Holy Spirit, the Lord and Giver of Life, who proceeds from the Father, who with the Father and the Son together is worshipped and glorified, who spoke by the Prophets;

And I believe in One Holy Catholic and Apostolic Church. I acknowledge one Baptism for the remission of sins. I look for the resurrection of the dead and the life of the world to come. Amen.

In All Seasons and in Every Hour

O Christ our God, who at all times and in every hour, in heaven and on earth, are worshiped and glorified; who are longsuffering, merciful, and compassionate; who love the righteous and show mercy to the sinner; who call all to salvation through the promise of blessings to come: O Lord, in this hour receive our humble prayers, and direct our lives according to Your commandments. Make holy our souls, bless our bodies, correct our thoughts, cleanse our minds; deliver us from all suffering, evil, and distress. Surround us with Your holy angels, that guided and guarded by them, we may hold onto the unity of the faith and to the knowledge of Your unapproachable glory, for You are blessed unto ages of ages. Amen.

The end of the day is another good time to add your own private devotions and prayers. Finish with the following prayer:

Through the prayers of our holy Fathers, Lord Jesus Christ our God, have mercy upon me and save me. Amen.

A Prayer before Sleep

Into Your hands, O Lord, I give my soul and my body. Bless me with Yourself, have mercy on me, and bless me with eternal life. Amen.

Saint Augustine's Evening Prayer

Watch, dear Lord, with those who wake, or watch, or weep tonight, and give Your angels charge over those who sleep. Tend Your sick ones, O Lord Christ, rest Your weary ones. Bless Your dying ones. Soothe Your suffering ones. Pity Your afflicted ones. Shield Your joyous ones. And all for Your love's sake. Amen.

On Watch
prayers for any time

Prayer is a great weapon, a rich treasure, a wealth that is never exhausted, an undisturbed refuge, a cause of tranquility, the root of a multitude of blessings, and their source.

—Saint John Chrysostom

Prayer is helpful in our daily lives. It is a powerful defense against the enemy when we make a prayer our own.

Lord, Have Mercy
When you have very little time for prayer, you can simply cross yourself and say,

Lord, have mercy!

The Jesus Prayer
In 1 Thessalonians 5:17, Saint Paul tells us to "pray without ceasing." The Jesus Prayer gives us a powerful tool to help us accomplish that mission.

Lord Jesus Christ, Son of God, have mercy on me, a sinner.

Prayer to Your Guardian Angel
O angel of God, my holy guardian, given to me from heaven, enlighten me this day and save me from all evil. Instruct me in doing good deeds, and set me on the path of salvation. Amen.

O angel of Christ, holy guardian and protector of my soul and body, forgive me everything wherein I have offended you every day of my life, and protect me from all influence and temptation of the evil one. May I never again anger God by my sins. Pray for me to the Lord, that He may make me worthy of the grace of the All-holy Trinity, and of the blessed Mother of God, and of all the saints. Amen.

Prayer to Your Patron Saint
Pray to God for me, O Holy Saint _____, for You are well-pleasing to God: for I turn to you, who are the speedy helper and intercessor for my soul.

Prayer to the All-Holy Trinity
The Father is my hope; the Son is my refuge; the Holy Spirit is my protector. O All-holy Trinity, glory to Thee.

Hymn to the Theotokos
It is truly meet to bless thee, O Theotokos, who art ever blessed and all-blameless and the mother of our God. More honorable than the cherubim and more glorious beyond compare than the seraphim, thou who without corruption barest God the Word, and art truly Theotokos: we magnify thee.

Prayer of Philaret, Metropolitan of Moscow
My Lord, I know not what I ought to ask of You. You and You alone know my needs. You love me more than I am able to love You. O Father, grant to me, Your servant, all that I cannot ask. For a cross I dare not ask, nor for consolation; I dare only to stand in Your presence. My heart is open to You. You see my needs, of which I myself am unaware. Behold and lift me up! In Your presence I stand, awed and silenced by Your will and Your judgments, into which my mind cannot penetrate. To You I offer myself as a sacrifice. No other desire is mine but to fulfill Your will. Teach me how to pray.

Psalm 141:2
Let my prayer be set before You as incense,
The lifting up of my hands as the evening sacrifice.

The Good, the Bad and the Family
prayers for relationships

Whoever sheds a fervent tear for the hardships of his fellow man, heals his own wounds.
—Saint Basil the Great

In the Bible there is a story of a man who was paralyzed but wanted desperately to see Jesus. Since he was unable to move himself, friends carried him to Jesus and lowered him through the rooftop so he could receive healing. When we pray for friends and family we are, in a way, carrying them to Jesus so they can receive healing, and, just like the friends of the paralytic, we receive a blessing because we participated in blessing them.

God wants us to bring not only our friends to Him, but our enemies as well. Matthew 5:44 tells us, "Love your enemies, bless those who curse you, do good to those who hate you, and pray for those who spitefully use you and persecute you." Our enemies are truly paralyzed and need to be carried by those who are strong, or they may never make it to Jesus for healing.

• *The story of the paralytic can be found in Mark 2:1–12.*

Prayer for a Sick Friend
(You may pray this for yourself too when you are sick.)
O holy Father, heavenly Physician of our souls and bodies, who have sent Your Only-begotten Son our Lord Jesus Christ to heal all our sicknesses and deliver us from death: Visit and heal Your servant _____, granting release from pain and restoration to health and energy, that *he/she* may give

thanks to You and bless Your holy Name, of the Father, and of the Son, and of the Holy Spirit, now and ever and unto ages of ages. Amen.

Prayer of a Child or Youth

Our Father who are in heaven, bless my father and mother, my guardians, and those who are in authority over me, for their love and tender care for me, and the blessings I receive at their hands. Help me, I pray, to be respectful and obedient to them in all things according to Your will; and give me Your grace to perform all my duties carefully and faithfully, to stay away from undesirable company and influences, and resist all temptation that may come my way; that I may live a well-governed, righteous, and godly life, ever praising You and glorifying Your Holy Name. Amen.

Prayer of a Single Person

O Blessed Lord, who have set up for us an example of ideal purity, strengthen me, I pray, when temptation attacks me, and when strong passions seek to overwhelm me, that I may remain constant in virtue and innocent in thought, word, and deed, doing such things as are well pleasing to You; grant me growth in wisdom and understanding, that I may serve You in holiness all the days of my life: through the intercessions of Your all-immaculate Mother and of all Your saints, especially my patron Saint _____. Amen.

Prayer for Friendships

Lord Jesus Christ, Savior and friend, I ask you to guide and guard my relationships with others. Allow Your hand to direct me in compassion, loyalty, and courtesy towards my friends. Guard my mouth and help me to be a good listener and offer words that encourage. Give me the strength of character to avoid participating in cruel or crude joking and hurtful attitudes. Keep me also from falling into sin by contributing to the sins of others by way of counsel, command, consent, challenge, or dare, praising their sin, hiding their sin, participating with them, silence, or defending their sin. Remind me to seek godly counsel when faced with difficult circumstances. Help me to be open when offering my friendship to others. Grant me Your mercy so that I can deal mercifully and wisely in all the situations that come my way. Amen.

Make a list of friends and other relationships you want to pray for/about:

_____	_____
_____	_____
_____	_____
_____	_____
_____	_____
_____	_____
_____	_____

Prayer for Enemies

Lord Jesus Christ, You who are just and offer freely Your forgiveness when I sin against You, help me now to offer that same forgiveness, even kindness, to those who do wrong to me. May my eager forgiveness to my enemies be a light to them so they too may come to know You. Let my actions speak of Your mercy and grace. May my words build up and not tear down. Guard my heart and mind against the temptation to seek revenge for wrongdoing. Remind me that each opportunity to practice the fruits of the spirit builds my faith and keeps my attention focused on You. Help me to love and show compassion toward my enemies, and let me see them as You see them. In the Name of the Father and the Son and the Holy Spirit, now and ever and unto ages of ages. Amen.

Make a list of those you are praying for:

_____	_____
_____	_____
_____	_____
_____	_____
_____	_____

Prayer for Family Relationships
(and for those who are home-schooled)

Almighty and merciful God, who formed me with Your loving hands, who knew before the foundation of the earth the family and situation in which I would live, I praise You and ask Your blessing on my interactions within my family. Give me patience when relating to my parents and siblings. Teach me to be a blessing through faithful, gracious service to each of them. Keep my mouth from criticism and complaining. Lead me away from selfish ambitions, but grant me close relationships built on trust and mutual honor. Help me in difficult times to avoid harboring bitterness or resentment, trusting that Your will and Your purpose will be accomplished. May I live sacrificially in my home as a testimony of your goodness. May they know by my actions that I am Your disciple. Grant me, O Lord, an attitude of gratitude, a mind that keeps no record of wrongs, a heart ready to forgive, and a heart that is not easily wounded. May it be for Your glory. Amen.

Make a list of immediate and extended family members you are praying for:

Prayer for One Who Is Dying—
by Saint Macrina the Younger
You, O Lord, have freed us from the fear of death. You have made the end of this life the beginning to us of true life. For a season, You rest our bodies in sleep and awake them again at the last trump. You give our earth, which You fashioned with Your hands, to the earth to keep in safety. One day You will take again what You have given, transfiguring with immortality and grace our mortal and unsightly remains.

Prayer for the Dead
(From the pocket prayer book)
Into Your hands, O Lord, I entrust the soul of Your servant _____, and call upon You to grant *him/her* rest in the place of Your rest, where all Your blessed saints rest, and where the light of Your face shines forever. And I ask also that our present lives be godly, sober, and blameless, that we too may be worthy to enter into Your heavenly Kingdom with those we love but see no longer: for You are the Resurrection and the Life, and the rest of Your departed servants, O Christ our God, and to You we give glory: to the Father and to the Son and to the Holy Spirit; now and ever and unto ages of ages. Amen.

Psalm 23—A Psalm of David
The LORD *is* my shepherd;
I shall not want.
He makes me to lie down in green pastures;
He leads me beside the still waters.
He restores my soul;
He leads me in the paths of righteousness
For His name's sake.
Yea, though I walk through the valley of the shadow of death,
I will fear no evil;
For You *are* with me;
Your rod and Your staff, they comfort me.
You prepare a table before me in the presence of my enemies;
You anoint my head with oil;

My cup runs over.
Surely goodness and mercy shall follow me
All the days of my life;
And I will dwell in the house of the LORD forever.

Prayer for the Departed—
From the Orthodox Funeral Service

Along with Your saints, O Christ, give rest to the soul of Your servant _____, in a place where there is neither pain, nor grief, nor longing, but life everlasting.

In the Hope of Resurrection

Be mindful, O Lord, of all those who have fallen asleep in the hope of resurrection unto life eternal, especially _____; pardon all their transgressions, both voluntary and involuntary, whether in word, or deed, or thought. Shelter them in a place of brightness, a place of verdure, a place of repose, whence all sickness, sorrow, and sighing have fled away, and where the sight of Your countenance rejoices all Your saints from all the ages. Grant them Your heavenly Kingdom, and a portion in Your ineffable and eternal blessings, and the enjoyment of Your unending life.

> *When mind and heart are united in prayer and the soul is wholly concentrated in a single desire for God, then the heart grows warm and the light of Christ begins to shine and fills the inward man with peace and joy. We should thank the Lord for everything and give ourselves up to His will; we should also offer Him all our thoughts and words, and strive to make everything serve only His good pleasure.*
>
> —Saint Seraphim of Sarov

Warning: Life Under Pressure
prayers for circumstances

When tested by some trial you should try to find out not why or through whom it came, but only how to endure it gratefully, without distress or rancor.
—Saint Mark the Ascetic

Prayer before Beginning Any Task

Almighty God, our help and protected hiding place, fountain of wisdom and tower of strength, who know that I can do nothing without Your direction and help; work with me, I pray, and direct me to godly wisdom and power, that I may complete this task, and anything else I may do, faithfully and enthusiastically, according to Your will, so that it may be beneficial to myself and others, and to the glory of Your Holy Name. For Yours is the Kingdom, and the power, and the glory, of the Father, and of the Son, and of the Holy Spirit, now and ever, and unto ages of ages. Amen.

Prayer before Going to School

O Lord my God, who love me so faithfully, bless each step I take this day. May my mind be full of Your truth and my mouth boldly speak Your praises. Enable me to stand as a light on my campus. Keep me from the temptation of peer pressure that would lead me in any direction contrary to Your will. Allow me to live a godly life balanced with grace and compassion, both in front of my peers and when no one is looking. Help me to avoid fruitless arguments or any kind of dispute. Direct me in all my dealings with peers and teachers to be honest, trustworthy, and hardworking. Keep me from any word or deed that would reflect negatively on my Lord. In the Name of the Father and of the Son and of the Holy Spirit. Amen.

Prayer before a Journey

O Lord Jesus Christ our God, the true and living way, be, O Master, my companion, guide, and guardian during my journey; deliver and protect me from all danger, misfortune, and temptation; that being so defended by Your divine power, I may have a peaceful and successful journey and arrive safely at my destination. For in You I put my trust and hope, and to You, together with Your Eternal Father and the All-holy Spirit, I ascribe all praise, honor, and glory, now and ever, and unto ages of ages. Amen.

Prayer in Times of Need

Almighty God, the Father of mercies and God of all comfort, come to my help and deliver me from this difficulty that besets me. I believe, Lord, that all trials of life are under Your care and that all things work for the good of those who love You. Take away from me fear, anxiety, and distress. Help me to face and endure my difficulty with faith, courage, and wisdom. Grant that this trial may bring me closer to You, for You are my rock and refuge, my comfort and hope, my delight and joy. I trust in Your love and compassion. Blessed is Your name, Father, Son, and Holy Spirit, now and forever. Amen.

Prayer when Facing the Unknown

O Lord, You who steadied the hand of Peter as he began to sink on the stormy sea, if You are with me, no one is against me. Grant to me the shield of faith and the mighty armor of the Holy Spirit to protect me and guide me to do Your will. The future I put into Your hands, O Lord, and I follow You to a life in Christ. Amen.

Prayer in Times of Trouble

O God, You who are my help in every situation, help me now in the trial I am facing. I thank You that I can trust You even when I don't understand what is going on. I thank You that You have a plan and purpose for my life, that You know how long this trial will last, and that I can live in confidence and not be afraid. Show me Your plan for this trial and how You want me to walk through it. Allow Your peace to rest upon my heart. Help me to give You glory and accept Your joy and grace throughout this time, for You are holy, righteous, and good. You alone are my hiding place and strong foundation that will not fall. Amen.

Thanksgiving after Deliverance from Trouble

Thank You, O Mighty God, for Your perfect help and deliverance from my trial. Help me to learn from this trial and to always remember Your faithfulness in every part of my life. Amen.

Declaration of Dependence
the sacrament of confession

My child, do you want to crush the head of the serpent?
Openly reveal your thoughts in confession. The strength of
the devil lies in cunning thoughts. Do you hold onto them?
He remains hidden. Do you bring them to the light? He
disappears. And then Christ rejoices, the prayer progresses,
and the light of grace heals and brings peace to your nous
and heart.

—Elder Joseph the Hesychast

Confession is a wonderful gift that frees us to serve God wholeheartedly and keeps us from deceiving ourselves. The Bible tells us in James 5:16, "Confess *your* trespasses to one another, and pray for one another, that you may be healed. The effective, fervent prayer of a righteous man avails much." Confession is a way of obtaining healing and helps to equip us for the righteous life God calls us to while bringing us back in union with Himself.

Now, we don't just go to confession and list off our top ten offenses. It's a time to prepare and clean out *all* the sinful areas in our lives that we are aware of and find those things we may not be aware of. Before going over the confession questions, spend some time in personal genuine prayer asking the Lord to give you the courage to confess, accept the healing He offers, and change your way of life to line up with His plan for you.

• **The Ten Commandments can be found in Exodus 20:1–17 in your Bible.**

+ One ~ Uno ~ Un ~ ενα

you shall have no other gods before Me

Many of us have gods in our lives that we don't even know about: money, popularity, fashion, possessions. Whatever we put above our devotion to the Lord is a god. When checking out this area of your life, ask the following:

Have I:
+ believed in God the Father, the Son, and the Holy Spirit?
+ trusted in God and His mercy?
+ complained against God when I am in trouble or having a hard time?
+ doubted the Christian faith and teachings of the Church?
+ believed in untrue, magical, or superstitious things?
+ gone often to religious meetings or festivals of those who do not follow the way of the Church?
+ not done what God wants me to do because I was afraid of being made fun of or picked on?

+ Two ~ Dos ~ Deux ~ δυο

you shall not make for yourself a carved image,
or any likeness of anything that is in heaven above,
or that is in the earth beneath,
or that is in the water under the earth

Okay, so you're probably not going to go out, find a piece of wood, carve it into an idol, and start worshipping it. But you might give too much attention to clothes, video games, movies, TV shows, famous people, and so forth. You may also have made yourself an idol when you put your desires or activities first in your life. The world teaches the "it's all about me" philosophy, but God tells us that it's all about Him.

> *He who refuses to give in to passions does the same as he who refuses to bow down and worship idols.*
> —Saint Theophan the Recluse

Have I:

+ made an idol out of any person, form of entertainment, or thing in my life?
+ glorified any person, place, or thing above the Lord?
+ kept my mind on Jesus' holy life and tried to imitate Him in my actions and relationships?
+ taken attention away from Jesus during church by talking to friends or only pretending to worship?
+ taken Holy Communion regularly, having my heart right with God and man?

+ Three ~ Tres ~ TROIS ~ τρια

you shall not take the name of the LORD your God in vain

This commandment is all about our words. Sometimes we unintentionally use the name of the Lord in an unholy way. We hear it all around us—with friends, in movies, on TV—but we still have to make a conscious choice not to sin in this way. We also "curse" the Lord when we speak badly of anyone, because all people are made in His image. We are badmouthing His creation when we participate in this kind of talk.

The Bible tells us the tongue is a very hard thing to tame, but as Christians we are called to step up to that challenge (James 1:26).

Have I:

+ used the Holy Name of God in a wrong way?
+ spoken badly to or about anyone?
+ made any promise that I didn't keep?
+ been reverent to holy things and people?

+ Four ~ Cuatro ~ QUATRE ~ τεσσερα

remember the Sabbath day, to keep it holy

The Sabbath isn't just any other day. Saint Maximos the Confessor says, "God ordained the honoring of the Sabbath, the months and festivals, not because He wanted these days to be honored by men as days, for that would be serving the creature more than the Creator (Romans 1:25), implying that days are naturally worthy of honor and therefore of worship in themselves. But through the ordinance to honor the days, He symbolically ordained the honoring of Himself. For He, Himself, is the Sabbath, the source of rest from the cares and labors of life. He is the Pascha, the Liberator of those held in the bitter servitude of sin; He is the Pentecost, the beginning and end of all."

Have I:

+ stayed away from church on Sundays or stopped others from going?
+ done unnecessary work on Sunday?
+ spent the Sabbath doing sinful things or behaved inappropriately?
+ kept the fasts and festivals as the Church instructs?

+ Five ~ Cinco ~ Cɪɴǫ ~ πεντε

honor your father and your mother

Honor is an important part of healthy relationships, especially within the family. Honoring your parents is a lifelong commitment. From childhood through the time we are on our own, we are under their authority and are called not only to honor them but to obey them as well. Even if we don't agree with them, we are to obey and honor them. This changes a bit when we are grown and out of their house and direct authority, but we are always called to honor our parents. Saint Cyril of Jerusalem says, "The first virtue of godliness in Christians is to honor their parents, to requite the troubles of those who begat them."

Have I:
+ joyfully and willingly respected my parents and been obedient to them?
+ been sneaky or lied to them or caused them pain by my words or actions?
+ failed to care for them or to help them?
+ kept up my responsibilities within my family and home?
+ been loving and kind towards my brothers and sisters? Have I harmed them in any way? Have I set a good example for them and offered encouragement? Have I approached them correctly when I have been offended, using patience, not anger?
+ worked for paid jobs with honesty and diligence?
+ honored God as my heavenly Father by treating others as my brothers and sisters?

+ Six ~ Seis ~ Six ~ εξι

you shall not murder

While it is not likely that you will ever need to confess the physical act of murder, we have to look at this commandment as it pertains to our hearts. The Lord says in Matthew 5:21–22, "You have heard that it was said to those of old, 'You shall not murder, and whoever murders will be in danger of the judgment.' But I say to you that whoever is angry with his brother without a cause shall be in danger of the judgment. And whoever says to his brother, 'Raca!' shall be in danger of the council. But whoever says, 'You fool!' shall be in danger of hell fire."

We must be cautious with our words, not in a hurry to take offense, and available to listen (James 1:19). Saint John Climacus says, "As with the appearance of light, darkness retreats; so, at the fragrance of humility, all anger and bitterness vanishes."

Have I:
+ caused the injury or death of anyone, or wished that I were dead?
+ enjoyed violent movies or video games?
+ given way to anger or harmed others with words or actions?
+ ignored others who needed help, or failed to stand up for those being treated badly by others?
+ been unkind to any person or creature?
+ imagined or pretended that I was hurting or killing someone?
+ failed to forgive anyone or held onto angry thoughts toward them?

+ Seven ~ Siete ~ SEPT ~ επτα

you shall not commit adultery

Transgressions against this commandment are hard to confess. The seventh commandment deals not only with the physical action of sex outside marriage, but also with what we read, listen to, look at in private, think, and do. Just as anger is murder in the heart, lust is adultery/sexual immorality in the heart. The Lord says in Matthew 5:28, "But I tell you that whoever looks at a woman to lust for her has already committed adultery with her in his heart." This applies to both males and females. If you're not sure whether your feelings fall into the category of lust, ask a parent or priest.

This commandment covers faithfulness in other areas of our lives as well—faithfulness to friends, family, and activities we agree to.

Have I:

+ had any inappropriate thoughts, said any inappropriate words, or done inappropriate things?
+ committed any sinful action alone or with others?
+ read any inappropriate books or magazines?
+ looked at inappropriate things on TV or on the internet?
+ fantasized about sex or told sexual jokes?
+ enjoyed listening to anyone talk about inappropriate things?
+ looked at sexual/pornographic websites?
+ been slothful, inactive, or wasted my time?
+ led others to do sinful things?

+ Mine Field!

There are many ways to participate in the sins of others without even knowing it. Look below to see if you're allowing the enemy to sabotage your walk.

You may hit a mine field if:

+ you encourage someone to sin
+ you force or require someone to do something sinful
+ you give permission to someone to engage in sin
+ you challenge or dare someone to sin
+ you show approval to others when they sin
+ you help hide someone's sin
+ you willingly participate in another's sin
+ you keep secret a sin that is dangerous to the person or to others
+ you defend the sin committed

Caution: It may not be "minding your own business" or loyalty to keep another person's sin silent. It may be active participation. It is difficult to know what to do in some situations. If someone has told you they have done something, or are about to do something, that will hurt themselves or others, it is wise to seek advice from an adult you trust. Keeping a secret is a sin if it results in harm to others.

+ Eight ~ Ocho ~ Huit ~ οκτω

you shall not steal

This commandment is pretty self-explanatory. What about the robberies that take place daily in our spending, with our possessions, and with our time? You decide where you stand.

Have I:

+ stolen anything or wanted to steal?
+ kept anything that didn't belong to me?
+ tried honestly to find owners of lost things I have found?
+ cheated anyone?
+ paid everyone what I owe them?
+ been wasteful with my money and possessions?
+ given to those in need?
+ used my time wisely?

+ Nine ~ Nueve ~ Neuf ~ εννεα

you shall not bear false witness against your neighbor

Just like the third commandment, this one deals with the tongue. James 1:26 says, "If anyone among you thinks he is religious, and does not bridle his tongue but deceives his own heart, this one's religion *is* useless." When we bear false witness against our neighbor (friends, family, enemies . . .) we tell the world that our faith is false.

> *A lie is the destruction of love, and a false oath is a denial of God.*
> —Saint John Climacus

Have I:

+ told lies or "enhanced" the truth?
+ made careless statements or spoken evil of anyone?
+ told any secrets (not including emergency or dangerous things) shared with me?
+ gossiped about anyone or made others think badly of someone?
+ covered up the truth in any way?

+ Ten ~ Diez ~ Dix ~ δεκα

you shall not covet your neighbor's house;
you shall not covet your neighbor's wife,
nor his male servant, nor his female servant, nor his ox,
nor his donkey, nor anything that is your neighbor's

Our world encourages us to want what everyone else has. It encourages us to follow our dreams by telling us to look to others and their possessions to determine what we want. God has another plan. He gives us what we need to make us who He knows we should be. In our effort to find ourselves, we discover that the only place we'll find complete fulfillment is in Christ. This commandment is all about it *not* being "all about me."

As for your own envy, you will be able to check it if you
rejoice with the man whom you envy whenever he rejoices,
and grieve whenever he grieves.
—Saint Maximos the Confessor

Have I:

+ envied anything good that has come to others?
+ been jealous about a good thing that has happened to someone else?
+ wished for anything that belonged to someone else?
+ damaged or destroyed anything that belongs to someone else?
+ wished for things God has not given me or been dissatisfied with what He has provided?
+ shared when I had the opportunity?
+ hoped for anyone to fail so I could get what they have?
+ failed to be kind and giving to others?
+ expected God to give me things when I refuse to give to others?

+ Demolition

The point of confession is to demolish anything in our lives that keeps us from serving God. The Ten Commandments help us eradicate the major obstacles we're most aware of. There are other sins, more like slow-release poisons, that are more subtle but just as deadly. Take an inventory of your heart and see if any of these poisons have penetrated your spiritual barricades.

+ **PRIDE:** assumption, big-headedness, cockiness, conceit, condescension, disdain, egotism, overconfidence, presumption, pretension, self-exaltation, self-importance, self-love, smugness, snobbery, swelled-head, vanity, "me"
+ **GREED:** covetousness, craving, eagerness, excess, gluttony, grabbiness, indulgence, insatiability, piggishness, ravenousness, selfishness, the "gimmes," voracity
+ **LUST:** carnality, covetousness, craving, envy, fancy, hankering for, itching for, longing for, lusting after
+ **ANGER:** animosity, annoyance, antagonism, blowing up, chagrin, displeasure, distemper, enmity, exasperation, fury, gall, hatred, impatience, indignation, infuriation, irritability, irritation, getting mad, outrage, passion, rage, resentment, tantrum, temper, violence
+ **GLUTTONY:** appetite, bellyful, excess, glut, overabundance, overflow, overindulgence, overkill, insatiability, oversaturation, superabundance, surplus, too much
+ **ENVY:** begrudge, covet, crave, desire, die over, hunger after, long for, lust after, resent, want, yearn for
+ **SLOTH:** apathy, idleness, inactivity, indolence, lethargy, neglectfulness, negligence, passivity, slackness, sleepiness, slowness, sluggishness

+ After Confession

Confession has a way of making the confessor feel clean. It's like taking a shower and washing away the caked-on mud of our sins. We need to remember that when we confess and our priest lays the stole over us, we are indeed forgiven. God tells us that He puts our sins away from Himself as far as the east is from the west, never to be remembered. It is our choice then to accept the forgiveness the King of the universe offers us, and to turn and make new life choices that will guard us from repeating those same sins.

Prayer after Confession

O almighty and merciful God, I truly thank You for the forgiveness of my sins; bless me, O Lord, and help me always, that I may ever do what is pleasing to You and sin no more. Amen.

+ Armed and Ready

Now that you've eradicated the major obstacles and poisons from your life, you'll want to guard the outpost of your heart. The enemy is always looking for ways to throw new obstacles in your path and deriving new poisons to cause death to your spirit. The following virtues are powerful weapons against the attacks of the enemy.

+ **HUMILITY**: blessedness, devotion, faith, godliness, grace, piety, purity, reverence, righteousness, saintliness
+ **LIBERALITY**: benevolence, charity, chivalry, compassion, consideration, courtesy, generosity, kindness, unselfishness

+ **CHASTITY**: abstinence, decency, innocence, integrity, maidenhood, modesty, monogamy, morality, purity, restraint, virginity, virtue
+ **MILDNESS**: agreeableness, amiability, attentiveness, attractiveness, charity, charm, cordiality, delightfulness, enjoyableness, gallantry, gentility, gratefulness, kindness, pleasantness, politeness
+ **TEMPERANCE**: abstinence, asceticism, control, discretion, forbearance, moderation, prudence, reasonableness, restraint, sacrifice, self-control, self-denial, self-discipline, sobriety
+ **HAPPINESS**: blessedness, cheerfulness, contentment, delight, elation, enjoyment, euphoria, exhilaration, exuberance, gladness, joy, laughter, light-heartedness, pleasure, prosperity, rejoicing, sanctity, vivacity, well-being
+ **DILIGENCE**: activity, application, assiduity, attentiveness, carefulness, constancy, earnestness, exertion, heedfulness, industry, intensity, keenness, laboriousness, perseverance

+ The Beatitudes—
Matthew 5:3–16

"Blessed *are* the poor in spirit,
For theirs is the kingdom of heaven.
Blessed *are* those who mourn,
For they shall be comforted.
Blessed *are* the meek,
For they shall inherit the earth.
Blessed *are* those who hunger and thirst for righteousness,
For they shall be filled.
Blessed *are* the merciful,
For they shall obtain mercy.

Blessed *are* the pure in heart,
For they shall see God.
Blessed *are* the peacemakers,
For they shall be called sons of God.
Blessed are those who are persecuted for righteousness' sake,
For theirs is the kingdom of heaven.

"Blessed are you when they revile and persecute you, and say all kinds of evil against you falsely for My sake. Rejoice and be exceedingly glad, for great *is* your reward in heaven, for so they persecuted the prophets who were before you.

"You are the salt of the earth; but if the salt loses its flavor, how shall it be seasoned? It is then good for nothing but to be thrown out and trampled underfoot by men. You are the light of the world. A city that is set on a hill cannot be hidden. Nor do they light a lamp and put it under a basket, but on a lampstand, and it gives light to all *who are* in the house. Let your light so shine before men, that they may see your good works and glorify your Father in heaven."

The Witness Stand
prayers with the Bible and the saints

We, as Christians, are here to be witnesses to the world of God's unfailing love and faithfulness. Your life may be the only Bible someone reads, your words the only church service they hear. God sheds His light on us as we trust in Him. We can either bring His light to a dark world or contribute to its darkness. The path we follow as Christians is very narrow and sometimes hard to see, but when we stand for Christ we do not stand alone. He stands with us. His Holy Word supports us. His holy saints pray for us. Knowing God's Word and imitating the lives of the saints will help us to be ready for whatever statement God wants our lives to make.

The following passages are for encouragement in different kinds of trouble. Please don't stop here, though. Your Bible is a wealth of history, tradition, encouragement, and power. Use the prayers below each verse or personalize your own prayers specifically to the trial you are facing.

+ Addiction

Ask Holy Martyr Boniface & the Righteous Aglais to pray on your behalf.

Checkpoint: An addiction can come from substance abuse, but also from unhealthy relationships or unhealthy situations.

Matthew 5:6

Blessed *are* those who hunger and thirst for righteousness, for they shall be filled.

Thank You, Lord, that You promise to fill me with Your holiness and satisfy my thirst with Your love.

John 8:32

And you shall know the truth, and the truth shall make you free.

Thank You, Lord, that Your Holy Word and One Holy Catholic and Apostolic Church offer the truth, that I may know You better and enjoy freedom through You.

John 8:36

Therefore if the Son makes you free, you shall be free indeed.

Help me, O Holy Trinity, to accept the freedom You offer.

Galatians 2:20

I have been crucified with Christ; it is no longer I who live, but Christ lives in me; and the *life* which I now live in the flesh I live by faith in the Son of God, who loved me and gave Himself for me.

Thank You, Jesus, that You have allowed me to share in Your death and Resurrection. Thank You that I can live by faith in You and depend on You completely.

+ Anger

Ask Saint Tikhon of Zadonsk to pray on your behalf.

Checkpoint: This is an area that many Christians struggle with to some degree. Anger does not always show itself in ranting and raving, breaking things, or generally freaking out. It may take root in our lives in smaller, less conspicuous ways. When we are angry at someone, it may show in our tone of voice, our unwillingness to show them acts of kindness, or in indifference or sarcasm. This last can be very destructive in relationships. Sarcasm can be funny and the anger it hides may go unnoticed by outsiders, but it can also be brutal. Saint John Climacus says, *"The first step toward freedom from anger is to keep the lips silent when the heart is stirred; the next, to keep thoughts silent when the soul is upset; the last, to be totally calm when unclean winds are blowing."*

1 Peter 2:23

[Christ], when He was reviled, did not revile in return; when He suffered, He did not threaten, but committed *Himself* to Him who judges righteously.

Lord, just as You held Your tongue and suffered, help me to do the same.

Ephesians 4:26–27

"Be angry, and do not sin": do not let the sun go down on your wrath, nor give place to the devil.

Dear Father who are in heaven, help me to speak with those I am angry with, now, in a loving way.

Proverbs 16:32

He who is slow to anger *is* better than the mighty,
And he who rules his spirit than he who takes a city.

O Holy Spirit, help me to rule my spirit in peace.

+ Anxiety/Depression

Ask Saint Anastasia to pray on your behalf.

> *The weather shifts from cloudy to clear and then back to rain; thus it is with human nature. One must always expect clouds to hide the sun sometimes. Even the saints have had their dark hours, days and weeks. They say then that "God has left them" in order that they may know truly how utterly wretched they are of themselves, without His support. These times of darkness, when all seems meaning-less, ridiculous and vain, when one is beset by doubt and temptations, are inevitable. But even these times can be harvested for good.*
>
> —*Way of the Ascetics*

Caution: If you think you are struggling with anxiety or depression, tell someone! Talk to your parents, priest, or counselor.

John 14:27

"Peace I leave with you, My peace I give to you; not as the world gives do I give to you. Let not your heart be troubled, neither let it be afraid."

Lord, grant me Your peace and help my heart not to be troubled.

Romans 8:28

And we know that all things work together for good to those who love God, to those who are the called according to *His* purpose.

Thank You, Lord, that You do work all things together for my good.

Philippians 4:5–8

> Let your gentleness be known to all men. The Lord *is* at hand. Be anxious for nothing, but in everything by prayer and supplication, with thanksgiving, let your requests be made known to God; and the peace of God, which surpasses all understanding, will guard your hearts and minds through Christ Jesus. Finally, brethren, whatever things are true, whatever things *are* noble, whatever things *are* just, whatever things *are* pure, whatever things *are* lovely, whatever things *are* of good report, if *there is* any virtue and if *there is* anything praiseworthy—meditate on these things.

Lord, allow your peace to surround me as I think on Your truth.

Psalm 46:1–2

> God *is* our refuge and strength,
> A very present help in trouble.
> Therefore we will not fear,
> Even though the earth be removed,
> And though the mountains be carried into the
>   midst of the sea.

Thank You, Lord, that You are my strength no matter what difficulty I am facing.

+ Backsliding
(Stepping away from God)

Ask Apostle Peter, who denied Christ three times, to pray on your behalf.

John 6:37

"All that the Father gives Me will come to Me, and the one who comes to Me I will by no means cast out."

Thank You, Christ my God, for never turning me away.

Psalm 51:10–12

Create in me a clean heart, O God,
And renew a steadfast spirit within me.
Do not cast me away from Your presence,
And do not take your Holy Spirit from me.
Restore to me the joy of Your salvation,
And uphold me *by Your* generous Spirit.

You can say this psalm as a prayer!

Proverbs 28:13

He who covers his sins will not prosper,
But whoever confesses and forsakes *them* will have mercy.

Lord, help me to quickly confess my sins that I may receive Your mercy.

+ Bitterness

Ask Prophet Jonah to pray on your behalf.

Ephesians 4:31

Let all bitterness, wrath, anger, clamor, and evil speaking be put away from you, with all malice.

Lord, teach me Your ways of peace and mercy so I can be a light to the world.

Hebrews 12:14–15

[Look] carefully lest anyone fall short of the grace of God; lest any root of bitterness springing up cause trouble, and by this many become defiled.

Holy Trinity, You alone know the heart. Show me any roots of bitterness in my life that need to be uprooted.

James 3:14–15

But if you have bitter envy and self-seeking in your hearts, do not boast and lie against the truth. This wisdom does not descend from above, but is earthly, sensual, demonic.

Lord, keep me from delighting in sinful thoughts and feelings, but rather humble me that I might find favor in Your sight.

+ Carnality
(Sinful Desires of the Flesh)

Ask Saint Mary of Egypt to pray on your behalf.

James 3:16

For where envy and self-seeking *exist,* confusion and every evil thing *are* there.

Lord, I surrender myself to You; lead me in Your way of humility and kindness.

Romans 6:6–9

[For we know] this, that our old man was crucified with *Him,* that the body of sin might be done away with, that we should no longer be slaves of sin. For he who has died has been freed from sin. Now if we died with Christ, we believe that we shall also live with Him, knowing that Christ, having been raised from the dead, dies no more. Death no longer has dominion over Him.

Holy Spirit, remind me constantly that I have been set free from the slavery of sin. Help me to walk in that freedom.

Galatians 2:20

I have been crucified with Christ; it is no longer I who live, but Christ lives in me; and the *life* which I now live in the flesh I live by faith in the Son of God, who loved me and gave Himself for me.

Thank You, Christ my God, that it is no longer I who live but You who live in me. Remind me of that truth as I make choices this day.

Ephesians 4:21–24

Put off, concerning your former conduct, the old man which grows corrupt according to the deceitful lusts, and be renewed in the spirit of your mind, and . . . put on the new man which was created according to God, in true righteousness and holiness.

Lord, renew my mind that all my attitudes and actions will mirror Your righteousness.

+ Chastity/Purity/Modesty

Ask Saint Katherine of Alexandria to pray on your behalf.

Checkpoint: This one is almost too hot to touch. The world tells us that we need to dress to express ourselves, live to gratify our desires, taste, feel, touch, and do everything that "feels" right to us. It tells us that being flirtatious and seductive are positive character traits. It tells us that we need to express our sexuality in whatever way feels good.

God tells us something different. God calls us to dress modestly, focusing on the fashion statement the heart is making. This isn't because He has no fashion sense, but because He knows what a precious gift you are. He also calls us to treat each other with "absolute purity," which will affect how we dress and how we treat the opposite sex. God formed our hearts and knows what will bless them and what will damage them. The areas of chastity, purity, and modesty are not easy to surrender to the Lord, but as we strive to live His way we will find blessings on the narrow road.

> *Every man who loves purity and chastity becomes the temple of God.*
> —Saint Ephrem the Syrian

1 Thessalonians 4:1–8

Finally then, brethren, we urge and exhort in the Lord Jesus that you should abound more and more, just as you received from us how you ought to walk and to please God; for you know what commandments we gave you through the Lord Jesus. For this is the will of God, your sanctification: that you should abstain from sexual immorality; that each of you should know how to possess his own vessel in sanctification and honor, not in passion of lust, like the Gentiles who do not know God; that no one should take advantage of and defraud his brother in this matter, because the Lord *is* the avenger of all such, as we also forewarned you and testified. For God did not call us to uncleanness, but in holiness.

Therefore he who rejects *this* does not reject man,
but God, who has also given us His Holy Spirit.

Holy Trinity, help me to follow the ways of the apostles and not the desires of the flesh. Help me to keep my body and emotions pure so I can experience all the blessings You have for me in Your timing.

1 Timothy 2:9–10

In like manner also, that the women adorn themselves in modest apparel, with propriety and moderation, not with braided hair or gold or pearls or
costly clothing, but, which is proper for women
professing godliness, with good works.

Lord, help me concern myself with inner beauty, and let my outer clothing testify to Your holiness and love.

1 Timothy 4:12

Let no one despise your youth, but be an example to
the believers in word, in conduct, in love, in spirit,
in faith, in purity.

Holy God, help me to be an example not only to the world, but also within my church, as I follow You on the narrow path. Guide my tongue, actions, motives, and desires in everything I do.

1 Timothy 5:1–2

Do not rebuke an older man, but exhort *him* as a
father, younger men as brothers, older women as
mothers, younger women as sisters, with all purity.

Lord, help me to treat the opposite sex in a holy way, "with all purity," building godly friendships. Thank You that I have a great opportunity to serve You, and help me to encourage others to live in purity.

+ Confusion/Doubt

Ask Apostle Thomas to pray on your behalf.

Isaiah 26:3

> You will keep *him* in perfect peace,
> *Whose* mind *is* stayed *on You*,
> Because he trusts in You.

Thank You, Lord, that You are not disappointed when I have doubts. Help me to trust You regardless of how I "feel."

1 Corinthians 14:33a

> For God is not *the author* of confusion but of peace.

Holy Spirit, grant me Your peace.

James 4:8

> Draw near to God and He will draw near to you. Cleanse *your* hands, *you* sinners; and purify *your* hearts, *you* double-minded.

Holy Trinity, help me to draw near to You and purify my heart.

Hebrews 10:32–39

> But recall the former days in which, after you were illuminated, you endured a great struggle with sufferings: partly while you were made a spectacle both by reproaches and tribulations, and partly while you became companions of those who were so treated; for you had compassion on me in my chains, and joyfully accepted the plundering of

your goods, knowing that you have a better and an enduring possession for yourselves in heaven. Therefore do not cast away your confidence, which has great reward. For you have need of endurance, so that after you have done the will of God, you may receive the promise:

> "For yet a little while,
> And He who is coming will come and will not tarry.
> Now the just shall live by faith;
> But if anyone draws back,
> My soul has no pleasure in him."

But we are not of those who draw back to perdition, but of those who believe to the saving of the soul.

Thank You, Lord, for Your promises to lead, protect, and strengthen me in my weakness. Help me to remember all Your great blessings when I feel confused or doubt holy things. Thank You that my confidence is not in myself, but in You!

+ Failure/Insecurity

Ask Prophet Moses to pray on your behalf.

Proverbs 24:16–18

> For a righteous *man* may fall seven times
> And rise again,
> But the wicked shall fall by calamity.
> Do not rejoice when your enemy falls,
> And do not let your heart be glad when he stumbles;
> Lest the LORD see it, and it displease Him,
> And He turn away His wrath from him.

Lord, help me to stand no matter what. Help me to be an encouragement to those who also struggle to stand.

Psalm 145:14–16

> The LORD upholds all who fall,
> And raises up all *who are* bowed down.
> The eyes of all look expectantly to You,
> And You give them their food in due season.
> You open Your hand
> And satisfy the desire of every living thing.

Thank You for lifting me up when I am weak.

2 Corinthians 3:4–5

> And we have such trust through Christ toward God.
> Not that we are sufficient of ourselves to think of
> anything as being from ourselves, but our sufficiency
> *is* from God.

*Thank You that I can be confident in You. Thank You that I don't
have to rely on my own strength or understanding. Help me to look to
You as my hiding place and strength.*

2 Thessalonians 3:3

> But the Lord is faithful, who will establish you and
> guard *you* from the evil one.

Thank You, Lord, for your protection from the evil one!

Psalm 91:3–7

> Surely He shall deliver you from the snare of
>   the fowler
> *And* from the perilous pestilence.
> He shall cover you with His feathers,
> And under His wings you shall take refuge;
> His truth *shall be your* shield and buckler.
> You shall not be afraid of the terror by night,

Nor of the arrow *that* flies by day,

Nor of the pestilence *that* walks in darkness,

Nor of the destruction *that* lays waste at noonday.

A thousand may fall at your side,

And ten thousand at your right hand;

But it shall not come near you.

Thank You, Lord, that You are trustworthy. Help me to trust Your faithfulness. Thank You that I am completely under Your mighty protection!

+ Gossip/Taming the Tongue

Ask Saint John Chrysostom to pray on your behalf.

Checkpoint: It's such a small part of the body, but it can cause some real problems! James 3:4–5 says, "Look also at ships: although they are so large and are driven by fierce winds, they are turned by a very small rudder wherever the pilot desires. Even so the tongue is a little member and boasts great things. See how great a forest a little fire kindles!"

In *The Ladder of Divine Ascent,* Saint John Climacus says, "Talkativeness is the throne of vainglory, on which it loves to show itself and make a display. Talkativeness is a sign of ignorance, a door to slander, a guide to jesting, a servant of falsehood, the ruin of godly conviction, a creator and summoner of hopelessness, a precursor of sleep, the dissipation of recollection, the abolition of watchfulness, the cooling of zeal, the darkening of prayer."

Proverbs 16:28

A perverse man sows strife,

And a whisperer separates the best of friends.

Lord, guard my tongue, that it may build up, not tear down.

Proverbs 20:19

He who goes about *as* a talebearer reveals secrets;
Therefore do not associate with one who flatters
    with his lips.

Remind me, O Lord, of Your Holy Word as a guide to righteousness.
Allow my words to be truthful and kind.

Romans 1:28–32

And even as they did not like to retain God in *their*
knowledge, God gave them over to a debased mind,
to do those things which are not fitting; being
filled with all unrighteousness, sexual immorality,
wickedness, covetousness, maliciousness; full of
envy, murder, strife, deceit, evil-mindedness; *they*
are whisperers, backbiters, haters of God, violent,
proud, boasters, inventors of evil things, disobedient
to parents, undiscerning, untrustworthy, unloving,
unforgiving, unmerciful; who, knowing the righteous judgment of God, that those who practice such
things are deserving of death, not only do the same
but also approve of those who practice them.

Holy Lord, guard my mind and tame my tongue that I may not sin
against You.

James 1:26

If anyone among you thinks he is religious, and does
not bridle his tongue but deceives his own heart,
this one's religion *is* useless.

O Lord, my God, help my words to lead others toward You, not away
from You.

+ Loneliness

Ask Saint Theophan the Recluse to pray on your behalf.

John 14:18

"I will not leave you orphans; I will come to you."

Thank You that I can trust You to always be with me. Thank You that I am never alone.

Psalm 147:3

He heals the brokenhearted
And binds up their wounds.

Thank You, Lord, that You heal my lonely heart. Help me to reach out and be friendly to others so they will not feel alone.

Psalm 141:2

Let my prayer be set before You *as* incense,
The lifting up of my hands *as* the evening
    sacrifice.

Thank You that my prayers are pleasing to You, and that You like to hear me call upon Your Holy Name.

+ Lust/Pride/Temptations

Ask Saint Mary of Egypt to pray on your behalf.

> *He who loves God cultivates pure prayer, driving out every passion that keeps him from it.*
>   —Saint Maximos the Confessor

Checkpoint: In this world the sins of lust and pride are glorified. Movies, magazines, books, internet, and friends often reinforce standards that are contrary to the word of God. Cultural preferences have a great, or not so great, influence on moral standards. It is tempting to simply go along with "the norm," but it is God's standard we are trying to follow.

Facing temptations and choosing to turn from them is not easy. Temptations, hard as they may seem, can be the very things that help us in our journey of salvation. If we want to be stronger, we must exercise. When muscles are strained by exercise, the muscle tissue actually breaks down in the body. It seems counterproductive! But when we have completed our exercise, the body rebuilds the muscle tissue so that it is even stronger than before. It is the same with our spiritual life. As we are tempted and those muscles of faith and perseverance are challenged, each victory produces stronger spiritual muscles!

2 Peter 2:7–9

> [If the Lord] delivered righteous Lot, *who was* oppressed by the filthy conduct of the wicked (for that righteous man, dwelling among them, tormented *his* righteous soul from day to day by seeing and hearing *their* lawless deeds)—*then* the Lord knows how to deliver the godly out of temptations and to reserve the unjust under punishment for the day of judgment.

Lord, rescue me from the things that tempt me. Thank You that nothing is too big for You to handle, and help me to bring all my trials to You.

Matthew 18:2–4

> Then Jesus called a little child to Him, set him in the midst of them, and said, "Assuredly, I say to you, unless you are converted and become as little children, you will by no means enter the kingdom of heaven. Therefore whoever humbles himself as

this little child is the greatest in the kingdom of heaven."

O Lord, I lay down my pride and come to You as a little child, with trust and obedience. Help me to remain humble and remember that all the good in my life is because of You.

Proverbs 27:1–2

Do not boast about tomorrow,
For you do not know what a day may bring forth.
Let another man praise you, and not your
    own mouth;
A stranger, and not your own lips.

Holy Trinity, help me to use my mouth to glorify You and not myself; for praise, glory, and honor belong to You.

Luke 18:11–14

"The Pharisee stood and prayed thus with himself, 'God, I thank You that I am not like other men— extortioners, unjust, adulterers, or even as this tax collector. I fast twice a week; I give tithes of all that I possess.'

"And the tax collector, standing afar off, would not so much as raise *his* eyes to heaven, but beat his breast, saying, 'God, be merciful to me a sinner!'

"I tell you, this man went down to his house justified *rather* than the other; for everyone who exalts himself will be humbled, and he who humbles himself will be exalted."

Remind me, O Lord, that I am nothing without You. Help me to be ever mindful of Your mercy upon me, a sinner.

James 1:2–4

My brethren, count it all joy when you fall into various trials, knowing that the testing of your faith produces patience. But let patience have its perfect work, that you may be perfect and complete, lacking nothing.

Thank You for the trials You allow in my life. Help me to accept them and look to You for the strength to endure them.

+ Suffering/Trials

Ask Saint Nicholas the Wonderworker to pray on your behalf.

Hebrews 5:8–9

Though He was a Son, *yet* He learned obedience by the things which He suffered. And having been perfected, He became the author of eternal salvation to all who obey Him.

Thank You that You are aware of all my troubles and I can trust You to be my guide through them.

James 1:12

Blessed *is* the man who endures temptation; for when he has been approved, he will receive the crown of life which the Lord has promised to those who love Him.

Help me to persevere under my current trial.

2 Corinthians 4:8–10

We are hard pressed on every side, yet not crushed; *we are* perplexed, but not in despair; persecuted, but not forsaken; struck down, but not destroyed—always carrying about in the body the dying of the Lord Jesus, that the life of Jesus also may be manifested in our body.

Keep me ever mindful, O Lord, of Your great protection when the enemy presses in on all sides. Thank You that nothing he attacks us with will succeed.

1 Peter 4:19

Therefore let those who suffer according to the will of God commit their souls *to Him* in doing good, as to a faithful Creator.

Help me to continue to do good even in this difficult circumstance.

2 Timothy 2:3

You therefore must endure hardship as a good soldier of Jesus Christ.

Give me courage, O gracious Lord, to stand firm during this trial.

1 Peter 4:12–13

Beloved, do not think it strange concerning the fiery trial which is to try you, as though some strange thing happened to you; but rejoice to the extent that you partake of Christ's sufferings, that when His glory is revealed, you may also be glad with exceeding joy.

Holy Trinity, help me to rejoice in the sufferings I face, keeping in mind that I am participating in Christ's suffering.

Psalm 34:17

The righteous cry out, and the LORD hears,
And delivers them out of all their troubles.

Thank You that You will deliver me from all my troubles. Help me to accept whichever ways You choose to accomplish this.

+ Worlòliness

Ask Apostle Zacchaeus or Saint Matthew to pray on your behalf.

Checkpoint: We often think that if we feel like we're different from everyone else, then something must be wrong with us. Jesus tells us that we are "strangers in a strange land." We were created for perfection, for life in the Garden of Eden, so we will never be satisfied by this world. However, when we look to the Lord, He will satisfy our hearts and our minds. He will not disappoint us.

1 John 2:15–17

> Do not love the world or the things in the world. If anyone loves the world, the love of the Father is not in him. For all that *is* in the world—the lust of the flesh, the lust of the eyes, and the pride of life—is not of the Father but is of the world. And the world is passing away, and the lust of it; but he who does the will of God abides forever.

O Father in heaven, help my heart to desire Your righteousness and not the things of this world.

Mark 4:18–20

> "Now these are the ones sown among thorns; *they are* the ones who hear the word, and the cares of this world, the deceitfulness of riches, and the desires for other things entering in choke the word, and

it becomes unfruitful. But these are the ones sown on good ground, those who hear the word, accept *it*, and bear fruit: some thirtyfold, some sixty, and some a hundred."

Let me be like the seed sown on good soil, hearing Your word and accepting it. Let my life produce crops for Your kingdom and Your glory.

1 John 5:5

Who is he who overcomes the world, but he who believes that Jesus is the Son of God?

Help me, O Lord, to overcome this world through belief in Christ my Lord. Help my thoughts, words, and actions to testify to that belief.

+ Scriptures for Meditation

+ Psalm 23
+ Psalm 91
+ Psalm 119
+ Hebrews 12
+ Ephesians 2:1–10
+ Philippians 2:1–11
+ Philippians 4:6–9
+ 2 Peter 1:3–11
+ Luke 6:27–36

When the Saints Go Marching In
some saints who pray for you

*God's saints are near to believing hearts and, like the truest
and kindest friends, are ready in a moment to help the faithful and pious who call upon them with faith and love.*
—Saint John of Kronstadt

We pray to the saints because God has provided them
as the "speedy helpers and intercessors" for our souls.
Whether you're standing directly in front of an icon or you're
out with friends, you can ask a saint to pray on your behalf.
The following is a brief list of saints you can ask to intercede
for you. Get to know them, learn their stories, and follow their
examples.

Prayer to Your Patron Saint
Pray to God for me, O Holy Saint _____, for you are well-
pleasing to God: for I turn to you, who are the speedy helper
and intercessor for my soul.

For Sickness:
+ Saint Seraphim of Sarov
+ Saint Lucia of Sicily
+ Saint Anastasia

For Patient Endurance during Trials:
+ The Three Holy Youths
+ Saint Eustathius Placidas and Family
+ Holy Forty-two Martyrs of Amorion

For Difficult Situations:

+ Saint David the Prophet, Psalmist, and King
+ Saints Cyrus and John of Alexandria

For Help in Distress, Poverty, Etc.

+ Saint Brigid of Kildare
+ Saint John the Almsgiver of Alexandria
+ Saint Xenia Fool for Christ of St. Petersburg

For Young People:

+ Saints Faith, Hope, and Charity
+ Saint Nicholas the Wonderworker
+ Saint Zoticus, Feeder of Orphans

For Finding Lost Things:

+ Saint Phanourios the Great Martyr
+ Saint Menas the Great Martyr of Egypt

For Help in Studies:

Three Hierarchs:

+ Saint Basil the Great
+ Saint John Chrysostom
+ Saint Gregory the Theologian

+ Stand in the Gap
Intercessory Prayer

> *"So I sought for a man among them who would make a wall, and stand in the gap before Me on behalf of the land, that I should not destroy it; but I found no one."*
> — Ezekiel 22:30

How many times do we say, "Lord, have mercy," without even thinking about it? Each Sunday we are reminded throughout the liturgy that we are standing in the gap for our fellow man. These prayers remind us of the privilege and responsibility we have to pray for our church, priests, public officials, and our world.

+ For the peace of God and the salvation of our souls, let us pray to the Lord.

+ For peace in the whole world, for the stability of the holy churches of God, and for the unity of all, let us pray to the Lord.

+ For our Metropolitan (*Name*), our Bishop (*Name*), the honorable presbyters, the deacons in the service of Christ, and all the clergy and laity, let us pray to the Lord.

+ For our country, the president, and all those in public service, let us pray to the Lord.

+ For this parish and city, for every city and town, and for the faithful who live in them, let us pray to the Lord.

+ For favorable weather, an abundance of the fruits of the earth, and temperate seasons, let us pray to the Lord.

+ For travelers by land, sea, and air, for the sick, the suffering, the captives, and for their salvation, let us pray to the Lord.

+ For our deliverance from all affliction, wrath, danger, and distress, let us pray to the Lord.

+ For a perfect, holy, peaceful, and sinless day, let us ask the Lord.

+ For an angel of peace, a faithful guide, a guardian of our souls and bodies, let us ask the Lord.

+ For forgiveness and remission of our sins and transgressions, let us ask the Lord.

+ For all that is good and beneficial to our souls, and for peace in the world, let us ask the Lord.
+ For the completion of our lives in peace and repentance, let us ask the Lord.
+ For a Christian end to our lives, peaceful, without shame and suffering, and for a good account before the awesome judgment seat of Christ, let us ask the Lord.
+ Remember also, Lord, those whom each of us calls to mind and all Your people.

Lord, have mercy!

Basic Training
the Christian Walk

+ Contending For
the Orthodox Faith:
The Map and the Compass

Being an Orthodox Christian can be difficult at times. Sometimes it's hard to have a ready answer for those who ask about our faith. Below are some of the questions you may be asked, or questions you may have yourself. The answers may help you to have a better understanding of your faith, your responsibility within your relationship to God, and the powerful heritage found in the Church.

Q: Don't we just need the Bible and nothing else to understand and follow God?

A: When you go on a journey, it is important to have both a map and a compass. The word of God is the map that God has given the world to lead us to Himself. He has chosen the Church to be the compass by which we are able to keep to the narrow path. Before we had the Bible, God Himself opened the minds of the prophets, and then the apostles, to the Holy Scriptures. It was through these men, and the church fathers who followed, that God chose to instruct His Church. Neither the Church nor the Scriptures is independent of the other. There are over 30,000 different Protestant denominations, all of which claim to follow Scripture alone (*sola scriptura*), but they don't all believe the same things.

When we neglect to look to the church fathers and tradition for the interpretation of Scripture, then we fall into the trap of relying on our own life experiences and limited understanding. What happens when two people reading the same portion of scripture come up with two separate interpretations? Whose interpretation is correct? Just as some countries may use a constitution as the standard when interpreting law, the Church uses the Living Tradition to determine the accuracy of any interpretation and understanding.

Q: What's the big deal about Mary?

A: Mary wasn't just some girl who happened to be in the right place at the right time; her role was more deliberate than that. We see in the genealogies mentioned in the Gospels that this young woman and her role had been planned from the beginning. Mary was essentially the first Christian, as she was the first to say "yes" to Christ. We do not worship her, but we do honor who she was and what she did. She is the *Theotokos* or "God-bearer." We honor her for saying yes and being the door by which the Church was born.

Q: Do you pray to the saints? Why?

A: When we pray to the saints, we are both asking them to pray for us and asking that they become active in our lives. Those who have gone on before us are known as the Church Triumphant, for they have finished the race victoriously. Those of us remaining are known as the Church Militant, because we are still in the heat of battle. In Revelation 5:8 we have the description of the saints in heaven bringing our prayers before the throne of God. When we ask the saints to pray for us, we are asking someone to pray who is no longer bound and limited by this world, but who can wholly devote him- or herself to prayer on behalf of those in this life.

In addition, saints can be active in our lives. This is a mystery. When God gives a living person grace to help another, the resulting good work is a product both of God's grace and the action of that person. Similarly, the saints in an unseen way are active on our behalf when we call on them. Some non-Orthodox have a problem with this because they think everyone who has died is "present with God" (see 2 Corinthians 5:8), and thus somehow no longer present with us. But the Orthodox Church teaches that God's presence is everywhere, so those who are "present with God" are present with us also, even if we cannot see them.

Q: Why can't just any Christian take Communion (the Eucharist) in an Orthodox church?

A: The Eucharist is never to be taken lightly. In Protestant churches, Communion is offered to any believer. What one believes, however, can be very different from one person to the next. One may believe that Jesus is the Christ and another may believe that He was simply a good guy. One may believe that Communion is truly the blood and body of Christ, while the next sees it as simply a reminder or even just a funny little tradition we keep doing. Some have even called it "the holy snack."

When Orthodox Christians take the Eucharist, they are boldly proclaiming the truth of what Christ demonstrated in Scripture when He said, "Take, eat; this is My body . . . this is My blood . . . which is shed for many" (Matthew 26:26–29). If we do not take the Eucharist seriously, we condemn ourselves

(1 Corinthians 11:27–32). The priest, then, is an important part of the Eucharist. He knows his flock and is able to help keep them from incurring that condemnation. But if a non-Orthodox person comes to church, however sincere, the priest does not know the condition of that person's heart and therefore must not take the risk of allowing that person to partake in an unworthy manner.

+ Getting through the Obstacle Course: What do I do if...

+   **I feel betrayed by a friend:** It's always hard when a friend betrays us, no matter what the reason. Relationships should be built on trust; if you find a friend is not trustworthy, you may not want to share special information with that person. The Bible tells us how to confront a friend that has betrayed us: "Moreover if your brother sins against you, go and tell him his fault between you and him alone. If he hears you, you have gained your brother. But if he will not hear, take with you one or two more, that 'by the mouth of two or three witnesses every word may be established.' And if he refuses to hear them, tell *it* to the church. But if he refuses even to hear the church, let him be to you like a heathen and a tax collector" (Matthew 18:15–17). Sometimes we feel betrayed when it was really just a misunderstanding. To know if you were betrayed, ask yourself the following questions: Did I make it clear that what I was sharing was private? Did I confide something that was dangerous to myself or someone else and would have caused harm if my friend hadn't told? The most important thing is to forgive this person, whether you continue to confide in them or not. God calls us to forgive.

+ **I don't think I can trust my priest:** First you need to consider why you think your priest may not be trustworthy. Is it because you have a hard time trusting, or has the priest shown himself to be untrustworthy? If your priest has shared information about you or someone else from a confession, the bishop will need to be informed. It would be wise to seek the counsel of your parents or a deacon if this action needs to be taken. Your priest has taken a vow, and if that vow has been broken his activities will need to be investigated by the deanery and the bishop. If your priest has acted inappropriately towards you or asked you to enter into a relationship with him, then you must tell an adult you trust immediately! If, however, you are just uncomfortable with the priest at your church, you do have the right to ask another priest to be your confessor and receive absolution from him. It's not bad if you have a personality clash with your priest or feel uncomfortable. The important thing is that you find a priest you feel comfortable with and continue in the Sacrament of Confession for the benefit of your soul.

+ **My parents aren't Christians. Do I have to obey them?** Scripture and tradition both address this question: "Children, obey your parents in the Lord, for this is right. 'Honor your father and mother,' which is the first commandment with promise: 'that it may be well with you and you may live long on the earth'" (Ephesians 6:1–3). "He who is obedient, is an imitator of Christ, and he who is proud and talks back is an imitator of the devil. So let us be careful, whom we are imitating, Christ or the devil. . . .

The so-called Christians must be true, in word and deed and not false, only in name" (Elder Joseph the Hesychast). God doesn't tell us to obey our parents only if they're Christians. He simply says to obey. It may be that your obedience will be a testimony of God's love for them. In rare situations, parents may act in a completely inappropriate manner and command their child to do something immoral or illegal. In those instances, you would need to call on *their* authorities by telling your priest or another trustworthy adult, or, in extreme cases, calling the police.

+ **I've committed a big sin and am afraid to tell anyone:** No sin is too great to confess to your priest. Think of Saint Paul, whose sins included the murder of God's people! And still the Lord wanted him to repent and follow Him. When we sin, the devil wants us to keep it hidden so we will not seek redemption through confession and forgiveness. Saint Photini (the woman at the well in John 4) knew this. Her sins were great. Her sins were such a big deal that she had to draw water at the well during the hottest part of the day when no one else was there. Everyone in the town despised her. But she found compassion and forgiveness from Christ, who came to the well and greeted her with compassion. She found that her "multitude of sins" were no match for His limitless mercy. She allowed all those dark things she had done to be brought into His light, and He willingly forgave. Tradition tells us that she not only told the whole village about what Jesus had done for her, but she and all seven of her children served Him boldly all the days of their lives.

+ **I keep committing the same sin over and over again:** You're in good company if you struggle here. Many Christians fall into this. They try so hard to resist, but somehow they fail. If we ask God to help us, why does it seem He sometimes doesn't answer? The Church has established the Sacrament of Confession as a powerful defense against perpetual sin. When we know we are going to confess before our priest, it is a strong encouragement to stand firm in the faith and turn away from "the sin which so easily ensnares us" (Hebrews 12:1). Your priest may also have some insight or instruction that will help. Saint John Climacus said, "Do not be surprised that you fall every day, do not give up, but stand your ground courageously. And assuredly, the angel who guards you will honor your patience."

+ **I think I'm in love:** You are starting a new journey in life. You may think everyone is wonderful one day and feel like everyone is against you the next. The feeling that many think is love is really more of a new awareness of the opposite sex. The boy that was icky or the girl that was gross last year now brings new feelings to the surface that are anything but bad. This is the right time to start taking note, in group settings, of what attributes you appreciate in friends of the opposite sex. I say "in group settings" because it gives you a chance to see how people interact with others, and it keeps you from forming a feelings-based attachment. The feeling of being in love is like new paint on a building. It looks nice for a while, but it's not what's holding the building together. God calls us to pure relationships, and at this stage in life friendships are the way to stay pure in thought and action. For now, keep your heart open and available for the one whom the Lord has chosen for you. Then when you are older, you will be able to enter into marriage without any regrets and without having given part of your heart to someone who had no right to it. You must consider, too, that the Lord may have other plans for you and want you to remain single. If you have a chance, ask a few adults who have been married for awhile how love as an action is different from love as a feeling, and whether they have any regrets from relationships they may have had before getting married.

+ **I really want to be in an intimate relationship:** God has created your body as a wonderful gift. If you bought a gift for someone for their birthday, you would wrap it and keep it safe just for them. You wouldn't open it for others to see or try on. The same is true of your body. It is a gift for you to give your future spouse alone. The Bible says, "All things are lawful for me, but all things are not helpful. All things are lawful for me, but I will not be brought under the power of any. Foods for the stomach and the stomach for foods, but God will destroy both it and them. Now the body *is* not for sexual immorality but for the Lord, and the Lord for the body" (1 Corinthians 6:12–13). There are many things that we *can* do, but not all things are beneficial. I can hit my finger with a hammer. I have the freedom to do that, but it does not benefit my body. I can ride my bike into a tree, but neither I nor the bike would benefit. If, however, I care for my body and treat it as the treasure God has created it to be, I will avoid much pain, guilt, shame, and many other consequences that come with abusing the act that was created to be practiced only in the sacrament of marriage. When you feel under pressure or tempted to give in, remember that all things God asks you to do *will* benefit you. Always. "Have courage, faith, hope and love in God, patience unto the end, to gain your immortal soul which the whole world is not equal to" (Elder Joseph the Hesychast).

+ **I'm making myself throw up or starving myself to lose weight:** This is a potentially life-threatening situation. You need to talk to your parents, priest, or some adult you can trust about this right away. We are to care for our bodies as "the temple of the Lord." "Or do you not know that your body is the temple of the Holy Spirit *who is* in you, whom you have from God, and you are not your own? For you were bought at a price; therefore glorify God in your body and in your spirit, which are God's" (1 Corinthians 6:19–20). We tear down the temple when we don't nourish it properly. Anorexia and bulimia can cause serious physical damage or even death! Anorexia skews your perception of yourself. You may look just right or too skinny to the rest of the world, but you'll only see yourself as fat. It is important to trust the words of those who love you when they tell you that you need help.

+ **My friend is depressed:** The best thing you can do for a depressed friend is to encourage him or her to talk to a safe adult. It is wonderful you are willing to be a friend, but depression can be a very serious thing. A parent, priest, teacher, counselor, or doctor can help determine the cause of the depression and offer appropriate assistance. Continue to encourage your friend and pray for him or her. Remind him or her of God's love. "Prayer is a remedy against grief and depression" (Abba Nilus).

+ **I'm so depressed I'm hurting myself or don't want to live:** This is a very serious situation. **Seek help immediately.** It is important to find an adult you can trust and tell them what you are doing or thinking. The enemy seeks to distort the view of Christ in you. The Bible tells us in John 10:10 that the enemy's purpose is to steal, kill, and destroy. He seeks to deceive and isolate you, making you believe that you have no purpose. But you are an icon of Christ, created in His image as His most valuable treasure. "[Be] confident of this very thing, that He who has begun a good work in you will complete *it* until the day of Jesus Christ" (Philippians 1:6). **Please seek help right away.** Christ's death on the cross tells the world how valuable you are to Him!

+ **I'm being pressured to drink or do drugs:** There are many things in your life that you will be tempted with. These things may be presented as "no big deal," or you may be put down for not trying them. "Friends" may even try to convince you that "everyone does it." Guess what? "Everyone" doesn't. Proverbs 14:12 and 16:25 both say, "There is a way *that seems* right to a man, / But its end *is* the way of death." We need to look at what life offers us from God's perspective, not the world's perspective. There are many things we, as Christians, need to choose not to do, even though it may seem like we're the only ones abstaining. "Enter by the narrow gate; for wide *is* the gate and broad *is* the way that leads to destruction, and there are many who go in by it. Because narrow *is* the gate and difficult is the way which leads to life, and there are few who find it" (Matthew 7:13–14). God calls us to righteousness, not to ruin our fun or to make us unpopular with our friends, but because His love for us is greater than anything this world can offer. He desires us to live life to the fullest and not limit ourselves by damaging our bodies with drugs or excessive drinking. Ephesians 5:17–18 sums it up well: "Therefore do not be unwise, but understand what the will of the Lord *is*. And do not be drunk with wine, in which is dissipation; but be filled with the Spirit."

+ **I can't control my anger:** Ephesians 4:26 says, "'Be angry and do not sin': do not let the sun go down on your wrath." The explanation of this in the Orthodox Study Bible, taken from the words of Saint John Chrysostom, is this: "If you fail to master your anger on the first day, then on the next and even sometimes for a whole year you will still be dragging it out. . . . Anger will cause us to suspect that words spoken in one sense were meant in another. And we will even do the same with gestures and every little thing. . . . Be angry with the devil and not your own member. This is why God has armed us with anger. Not that we should thrust the sword against our own bodies, but that we should baptize the whole blade in the devil's breast." It's hard to imagine we can love those who frustrate us. The Bible tells us to love our enemies. It's easy to love those who are kind to us, but it takes courage and a deliberate choice to love our enemies. We may not like them, but we need to look at them as icons of Christ, just as we are. God calls us to do things differently from the world. The closer we walk with Him, the narrower the path becomes, but the more secure the ground and the more steady our feet. "If it is possible, as much as depends on you, live peaceably with all men" (Romans 12:18).

+ **I'm anxious all the time:** Anxiety, like depression, is a trial you need to tell someone about. In our media-enhanced culture, people have access to many more things to be worried about than ever before. If we have the flu, we can go online and wrongly diagnose ourselves with any number of fatal diseases with the same symptoms. Movies and books may also contribute to the feeling of anxiety. Philippians 4:8 says, "Finally, brethren, whatever things *are* true, whatever things *are* noble, whatever things *are* just, whatever things *are* pure, whatever things *are* lovely, whatever things *are* of good report, if *there is* any virtue and if *there is* anything praiseworthy—meditate on these things." There is a lot of "traffic" going on in our minds. We play out the "what ifs" as if they were real. God tells us to stop the traffic and purposely focus on the truth. He wants us to direct our minds to those things that are good, pure, noble, and holy. When we put into our minds things that do not honor the Lord, it is like providing ammunition for the enemy to use later. "It is well known how powerfully corrupt images act upon the soul, no matter in what form they may touch it! How unfortunate is the child who, closing his eyes, or being left alone and going within himself, is stifled by a multitude of improper images—vain, tempting, breathing of the passions. This is the same thing for the soul as smoke is for the head" (Saint Theophan the Recluse). Another common cause for anxiety among Christians is really more of a "something's not right" feeling. You can't quite put your finger on it, but something isn't right. Well . . . something *isn't* right. We were created for perfection in the Garden of Eden. We were created to live perfect lives free from sin and death and fear. The world in which we live is not the one we were created for. *But* Christ came to the world so that we would be saved from sin and death and fear. We just have to hold on and keep running the race.

+ **I'm having a hard time believing in God:** It is hard to believe in someone it seems we cannot see. Think of the apostle Thomas, who was *with* Jesus and saw Him raise Lazarus from the dead. Saw Him heal the blind and sick. Saw Him walk on water, and yet he doubted. John 20 tells us that even though Peter and John came back to tell the other disciples they had seen Jesus, Thomas said he wouldn't believe unless he could actually touch Jesus' wounds. Jesus gave him that opportunity when He appeared to all the disciples. He wasn't angry at Thomas for not believing. God tells us that if we seek Him, we will find Him. He promises to show you that He is who He says He is. "If any of you lacks wisdom, let him ask of God, who gives to all liberally and without reproach, and it will be given to him. But let him ask in faith, with no doubting, for he who doubts is like a wave of the sea driven and tossed by the wind. For let not that man suppose that he will receive anything from the Lord" (James 1:5–7).

+ **I can't forgive:** Sometimes forgiveness is very hard to grant. Sometimes people hurt us so deeply. But when we choose not to forgive someone, it's as if we're taking poison and waiting for them to get sick. We deceive ourselves with this thinking, because we are only hurting ourselves. "For if you forgive men their trespasses, your heavenly Father will also forgive you. But if you do not forgive men their trespasses, neither will your Father forgive your trespasses" (Matthew 6:14–15). When we forgive the offenses of others toward us, we humble ourselves to accept the forgiveness God has for us when we sin against Him. When we won't forgive the misdeeds of others, we are telling God there are things that shouldn't be forgiven. We become the judge. Every time we meet at church, we say the Lord's Prayer (found in Matthew 6:9–13). This is to remind us that we are to freely forgive, just as the Lord freely forgives us. You may not be able to trust that person again, but you can choose to forgive them. If you pray for the strength to forgive, God will give you the ability to do it, and your healing will begin.

+ **Someone is hurting me:** Abuse can take many shapes and sizes. If someone is hurting you physically or touching you inappropriately, tell a safe adult right away. If the first person you tell doesn't believe you, keep telling until someone does. No one has the right to hurt your body or mind in any way. Sometimes an abusive person will apologize sincerely after each incidence of abuse, but then abuse again. While you should forgive them, you cannot allow them to continue. There are many reasons a person will abuse another. Perhaps they were abused themselves. Maybe they like the feeling of control they experience. Whatever the reason, it does not excuse the sin they are committing against you. You may experience shame, anger, distrust, fear, and many other emotions. Don't let those feelings keep you from protecting yourself and getting the help you need. One thing you must do, so you do not remain in emotional bondage, is choose to forgive your oppressor. You may need your priest or a counselor to help you work through all the feelings you have toward the person who has hurt you. Healing isn't something that just happens overnight. If you cut your finger, you may bandage it, but it still takes time for the wound to heal. Christ alone can bring that healing to your mind and heart. "Every minute God forgives us, we should forgive one another. This is the greatest virtue, if you say: My God forgive my brother for whatever he did to me" (Saint Anthimos of Chios).

+ **I don't think my parents' rules are fair:** You're not alone on this one. There are very few teens who think their parents' rules are fair. Growing up in someone else's home, having to follow someone else's rules, is our first challenge course. Galatians 5:22 gives us a list of virtues called the fruits of the Spirit which are beneficial for our future lives. Each one of these virtues can be developed in our home. *Love:* loving our parents and siblings whether they deserve it or not, just as Christ loves us. *Joy:* a happy face can bring joy to those in our home. *Peace:* keeping our hearts peaceful in the midst of adversity. *Patience:* when the rules don't make sense or really aren't fair. *Kindness:* giving our parents the honor they deserve simply because God has placed them as our authorities. *Goodness:* blessing our parents through our obedience to them. *Gentleness:* keeping our attitudes and tone of voice in check when communicating in our family. *Faithfulness:* being trustworthy in our family and not complaining about our family to others. *Self-control:* practicing all of the above, not because it is easy, but because it is right. God doesn't call us to what is easy, but He does say He will help us with our trials.

+ **I see someone do something dangerous or illegal. What is my responsibility:** When you see someone do something dangerous or illegal, it is important to tell someone. If it is not safe for you to confront the person, or it could be a danger to you if the person found out that you told, please tell a safe adult anonymously, by phone or note.

In Closing
at Ease

You are no longer a young child. It is time to look to the Lord yourself, to choose Him above all things. It is time for you to hear and be heard. May the Lord bless you in your devotion to Him who called you into being.

Lord, I call upon Thee, hear me; hear me, O Lord. Lord, I call upon Thee, hear me; receive the voice of my prayer, when I call upon Thee. Hear me, O Lord.

About the Author

Annalisa Boyd, home-schooling mother of a few teens and tweens of her own, wrote this book to inspire and challenge Orthodox youth while encouraging personal faith within the community of the Church.

Annalisa resides in the foothills of the beautiful Rocky Mountains in Colorado with her husband and six children.

Young Adult Books
by Conciliar Press

The books listed on the following pages are available from Conciliar Press Ministries or from your local bookstore. Prices were current as of 10/1/2007, but are subject to change. Prices do not include applicable tax or postage and handling.

Please visit our website (www.conciliarpress.com) or call toll-free (800-967-7377) for complete ordering information or to place a credit card order.

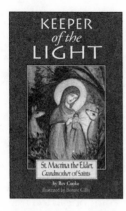

Keeper of the Light:
Saint Macrina the Elder, Grandmother of Saints

by Bev. Cooke,
with illustrations
by Bonnie Gillis

The road to sainthood takes a lifetime to travel. . . . Late in the fourth century, Christians are labeled enemies of the Roman Empire—hounded, arrested, tortured, and executed. Macrina and her husband Basil, once-wealthy Christians, flee with their small son to the mountainous forests south of the Black Sea. There, Macrina embarks on a seven-year journey of unexpected tests and trials that will take her through a harsh and hungry wilderness pilgrimage, only to plunge her into poverty and danger on the streets of Neocaesarea. So begins Macrina's adventure in faith, as she undertakes the process of becoming one of the most influential women in sacred history, the mother and grandmother of saints. Readers of all ages will be fascinated by the story of St. Macrina the Elder, who had a profound influence on her grandchildren—St. Basil the Great, St. Gregory of Nyssa, and St. Macrina the Younger. She is truly a great confessor of the Orthodox Christian faith. **A chapter book, with black-and-white illustrations.**

Paperback, 200 pages
ISBN 978-1-888212-77-8 • Order No. 007106—$14.95*

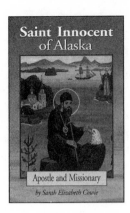

Saint Innocent of Alaska:

Apostle and Missionary

by Sarah Elizabeth Cowie

If you close your eyes and think about Alaska, what do you see? Eskimos and igloos? Mountains of snow? Polar bears and icebergs? Do you know that not all Alaskan natives are Eskimos? There are many different tribes of native peoples. Each has its own language and way of life. Many of these native peoples have been Orthodox Christians for over two hundred years. This is largely due to the missionary efforts of one man, Saint Innocent of Alaska. He converted and baptized thousands of native people into the Christian faith. He was a wonderful and godly man who lived a missionary life full of adventures that you would never dream of! Many people believe he is the greatest Christian missionary of all time. **A chapter book, with black-and-white illustrations.**

Paperback, 104 pages

ISBN 978-1-888212-74-7 · Order No. 006975—$10.95*

Ella's Story:
The Duchess Who Became a Saint

by Maria Tobias,
with illustrations
by Bonnie Gillis

Ella's Story brings to life the amazing journey of Princess Elizabeth, from privileged childhood to eventual martyrdom. While her biography, as St. Elizabeth the New Martyr, is available to adults, this is the first such book for girls, written in an approachable, appealing style. Maria Tobias tells the princess' story in such a lively way that the book is hard to put down. Elizabeth, a real princess, is gifted with all those qualities girls still seek (intelligence, beauty, wealth, renown), converts to Orthodoxy, and subsequently sheds all earthly glory for the greater prize of the martyr's crown. She is a true role model for today. **A chapter book, with black-and-white illustrations.**

Paperback, 80 pages
ISBN 978-1-888212-70-9 • Order No. 006536—$8.95*

Basil's Search For Miracles

A Novel

by Heather Zydek

Basil, an ordinary 12-year-old who dreams of being a reporter, is on a quest—he must find and report on true, modern miracles for his school paper, *St. Norbert's News*. After Basil sees a real weeping icon, meets with people who have been miraculously healed of deadly illnesses, and more, he begins to understand his faith and put it in motion in his own life. He struggles to get along better with his single mom, and befriends the social outcast of the school, a silent boy named Anthony. Throughout his first year at a private parochial school, Basil not only researches a new miracle for each issue of the *News*, but also learns that everyday miracles can happen even in his own life.

"Basil's Search for Miracles is a wonderful story, weaving religious mystery and understated suspense into a classic coming-of-age drama. I couldn't put it down." —Jason Boyett, author of *Pocket Guide to the Bible* and *A Guy's Guide to Life: How to Become a Man in 208 Pages or Less*

Paperback, 160 pages
ISBN 978-1-888212-86-0 • Order No. 007271—$13.95*